EX LIBRIS

UNIVERSITATIS SANCTI JOANNIS

Sketching Outdoors in Winter

Snowy Owl — Back & profile

Feb 1, 1987

ALSO BY JIM ARNOSKY

Sketching Outdoors
in Winter

BY JIM ARNOSKY

LOTHROP, LEE & SHEPARD BOOKS   NEW YORK

This season is dedicated to

PAUL GALDONE

Copyright © 1988 by Jim Arnosky

First Edition   1 2 3 4 5 6 7 8 9 10

Library of Congress Cataloging in Publication Data
Arnosky, Jim. Sketching outdoors in winter / by Jim Arnosky.
p.   cm. Summary: Provides drawings of landscapes, plants, animals, and other aspects of nature, accompanied by comments from the artist on how and why he drew them. ISBN 0-688-06290-3 : 1. Drawing—Technique—Juvenile literature. 2. Landscape in art—Juvenile literature. 3. Animals in art—Juvenile literature. 4. Nature (Aesthetics)—Juvenile literature. [1. Nature (Aesthetics) 2. Landscape drawing—Technique. 3. Animal painting and illustration—Technique. 4. Drawing—Technique.] I. Title.
NC735.A76   1988 743'.836—dc19   88-2202 CIP AC

The outward shows of sky and earth,
Of hill and valley, he has viewed;
And impulses of deeper birth
Have come to him in solitude.

WILLIAM WORDSWORTH
"A Poet's Epitaph"

INTRODUCTION

Winter is the season of limited light, cold temperatures, and snow. Where I live, the first snow usually falls soon after Thanksgiving. By the end of the year the whole countryside is under a deep blanket of snow. All of my winter sketching was done outdoors in the snow.

I worked on sun-warmed afternoons. I also ventured out in wet white storms and dry subzero weather. In looking over this book I see that some of my favorite sketches are those in which the lines record a slight shiver in their making.

I was comfortable most of the time I was outdoors sketching. I dressed warmly in clothing that could be removed layer by layer when the weather or the wearer warmed up, or added when I felt cold. I wore woolen gloves and took care to keep them dry. It is difficult to draw when your hands are cold and wet.

In addition to drawing materials I carried binoculars for watching wildlife, a portable wooden easel, a folding stool, and a hunter's "hot seat" cushion.

Whenever possible I sat in sunlight. When sketching out in open windy places, I wore a face mask and learned to squat down in the warmer windless snowhole made by my own body. In the woods, where in many areas snow lay four feet deep and more, I sketched standing on the supportive webbing of the snowshoes I had trekked in on.

In winter, just getting to a particular drawing subject or vantage point is an adventure. You feel the exhilaration of cold air on your face and in your lungs. Winter makes you think of essential things—warm life and cold death. It is the season to sketch solitary subjects. Against winter's stark background, everything stands out as strikingly individual.

Jim Arnosky
Ramtails
Winter, 1987

On December 24 I hiked to the top of the ancient quarry behind our place to sketch the view. The quarry is a familiar spot to me and just as familiar a scene. Yet as I sketched I discovered it all anew, from the great granite boulders in the foreground and our farm directly below, to the wooded hills across the way.

When sketching familiar scenes, you may feel tempted to add details you know exist, even though from where you are sitting they cannot be seen. Train yourself to include in your sketches only those details you can actually see.

After shading a dark wooded area, I use the thin edge of my eraser to create light-colored trees.

You can keep your kneadable eraser soft and pliable even in the coldest weather simply by carrying it inside your glove next to your warm palm.

Dec. 24.
24°.
Rantoul in Winter JEA

9

I made this drawing on Christmas Day. A warm storm was moving in. The air was damp with drizzling rain. The little evergreen tree's top was sticking up out of two feet of packed snow. This spot is not far from a village, and while I worked I could hear spirited rounds of rifle fire. Someone had received a new gun as a gift.

During winter the hours of light are few. Don't waste precious light searching for the "perfect" drawing subject. I chose this subject quickly—almost at random—from among the many evergreens in the area.

Everything in nature is unique and interesting to draw.

When sketching in a drizzling rain, or even in sleeting snow, you can keep your work in progress clean and dry by holding another sheet of paper tentlike over your drawing paper.

Notice the way the thorns on this berry stem point downward. Thorns hook onto things, which helps support the stem. Not all plant thorns hook downward, though. Look for small details like this when you are sketching thorny stems.

Evergreen and Berry Stem
in Snow
Christmas Day
SEA

11

Hornet Nest
Dec. 27
Jim Arnosky

Last summer some bald-faced hornets built their nest in the lilac bushes growing just outside our bedroom window. The lilac greenery had hidden the nest so well that we didn't know it was there until the leaves had fallen away. The nest in winter hangs exposed and devoid of life. The hornets have died—all except the mated females, which are hibernating in the ground now buried under snow.

To shade the nest surface, I used circular lines that suggest the crescent-shaped patterns the hornets themselves made.

To keep my nest looking as lightweight as the real nest, I simply avoided making heavy outlines. In drawings, heavy outlines suggest the strong pull of gravity.

Sketch all stems first, then add branches and twigs.

If a stem or branch appears dark and featureless, draw it looking that way. If a stem or branch is light in color and shows texture, modeling, and details, make it look so in your sketch.

After discovering the hornets' nest, I went on a small expedition to see what else the leafless trees revealed. In the brushy borders of fields, all around the pond, and along the riverbank, I spotted bird nests of various shapes and sizes. The abandoned nests appeared as dark clumps amid the slender lines of bare stems and branches. The most evident nests were those in trees or bushes that happened to be silhouetted against the white snow or light sky.

Do not handle bird nests. They could be harboring parasites.

As you look at a nest, try to identify the various materials it is made of. Birds use grasses, pine needles, twigs, mosses, leaf parts, animal fibers, and even spiderwebs in their nests.

Sharpen your pencil point for drawing fine materials such as hairs and spiderwebs. Use a duller point when sketching coarse and fibrous mosses, twigs, and grass blades.

When you are sketching a nest from nature, depict clearly all the materials you can identify. The rest can be suggested with lines and shading.

After you have added shading, use your eraser to "lift out" light-colored details such as grass blades or leaf pieces.

Bird nest in the
crotch of a small tree
Dec. 29 1986
29°

15

When you spend a day outdoors sketching bird nests, you come home carrying little pieces of wherever you have been. Clinging to clothing are seeds, thorns, slivers of bark, broken brittle branch tips, and fragments of dead leaves—all picked up while you were climbing and crawling through thickets where birds have raised their young.

Nest drawn actual size
Dec. 30 1986

16

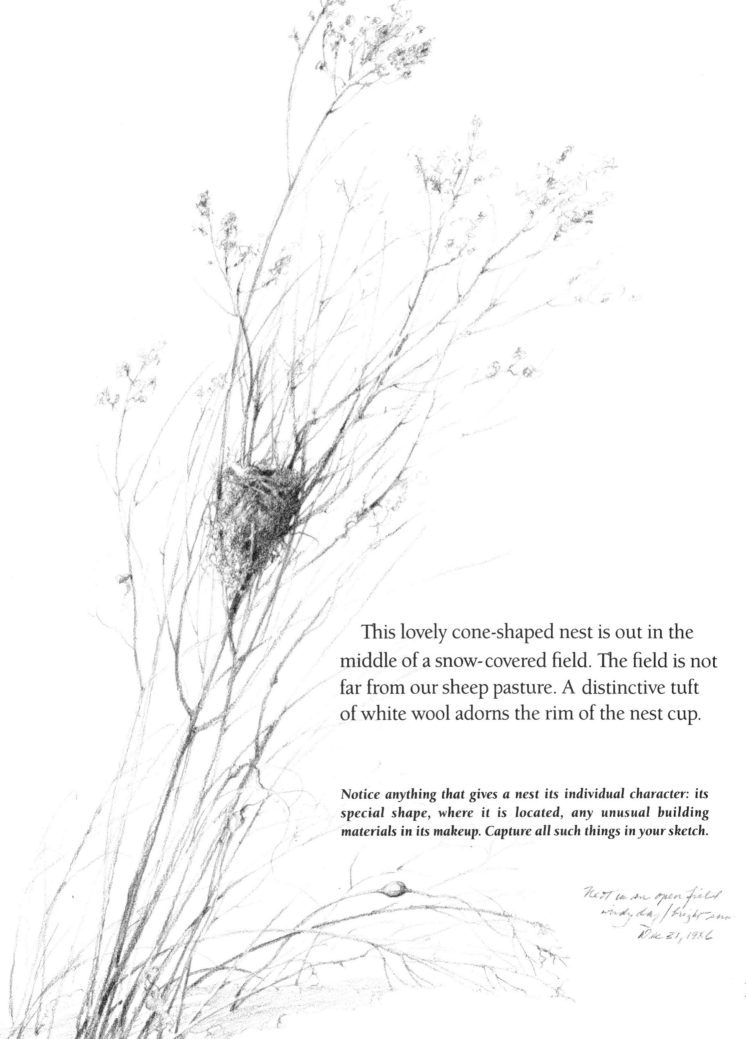

This lovely cone-shaped nest is out in the middle of a snow-covered field. The field is not far from our sheep pasture. A distinctive tuft of white wool adorns the rim of the nest cup.

Notice anything that gives a nest its individual character: its special shape, where it is located, any unusual building materials in its makeup. Capture all such things in your sketch.

*Nest in an open field
windy day / bright sun
Dec. 31, 1986*

Jim Arnosky
Hunting camps in Snowstorm
Jan 1987

I began this sketch of a friend's hunting camp just as snow was beginning to blow in from the north. At first the flakes were light and dry and flying horizontally. Very few alighted on my drawing paper. But as the storm grew stronger, bigger and wetter snowflakes began landing all over my work. I continued sketching, though, simply drawing my lines through the accumulating slush.

As long as you are warm and dry, keep sketching. It is surprising how well a picture can turn out under even the sloppiest circumstances.

Forgive any blurriness caused by snowflakes alighting on your lines.

When sketching a storm, make all shading lines follow the same direction the wind is blowing.

As long as your paper remains dry, you can use your eraser for making corrections, adding highlights, and lifting out small white spots that suggest snowflakes. But once your paper becomes wet, your eraser will be useless. It will only smear and smudge your pencil lines into the paper's soggy surface.

Back home I gave this sketch a more snowy look by spritzing white spots onto it. I dipped an old toothbrush in white paint, held the brush over my sketch, and then ran my thumb slowly over the wet bristles. The white paint spattered onto the page.

The morning after the storm I startled a band of blue jays that had discovered the unoccupied hornet nest and were tearing away its papery walls. The jays were searching for hornet carcasses or egg remains—meager pickings at best, but some food at least for hungry birds.

The blue jays had been going at the nest with gusto. Gray flaky pieces of nest lay all around on the snow. The birds had opened a large hole in one side, exposing the nest's center section of delicate comb. Seeing the nest's interior design, I was reminded of how often we do not fully appreciate the care and work that go into an object until we witness it being destroyed.

Notice the icicles hanging on the bottom of the nest. Icicles are formed when water dripping from an object freezes before it can fall away. Draw icicles as dripping water frozen in place.

Hornet nest after storm
and Blue Jay damage

Gordon Morrison
Jan 4 1987

21

On a very cold January day, seeking to sketch in a more remote setting, I followed a trapper's trail in the snow down a steep woodland hollow. The trail led to a large beaver pond that was frozen over and covered with snow. The trapper's boot prints made a wide circle around the beavers' lodge. In the course of that circle three traps had been set down in holes chopped through the ice. Each trap was wired to a pole that stood up ominously out of the hole.

I had done a number of quick sketches of the lodge and was walking on the pond looking for another vantage point when, suddenly, the ice under me broke and I plunged into the cold black water. As I scrambled up and out of the terrible hole, my soaked pants began to freeze. The experience was as frightening as the trek back out of the woods was uncomfortable. If I had fallen into slightly deeper water and not been able to climb out onto the thin ice, the sketched scene shown here could have been my last.

During winter, serenity and danger rest together in the cold. Be careful outdoors. Dress warmly. Don't take chances. Stay safe.

On long hikes through snow country you can quickly burn up the calories you consumed at breakfast. Take some lunch along to refuel the furnace inside you.

When sitting in the cold, keep your head, ears, neck, chest, and back covered, even if the sunlight feels warm. Winter wind, however slight, chills everything in its path. Body heat drawn off by cold air cannot readily be regained.

Bear Lodge lodgepole pines
JEA 1987

23

The quarry property behind our farm is mostly woodland surrounding a huge hole. The hole is the result of many blastings to obtain rock that was used for building roads, bridge shoulders, cellars, and monuments. There is a place down in the quarry where you can stand and look up at the gray granite walls. It is a natural cathedral with a ceiling of light during the day and a dome of stars at night.

When sketching snow scenes, avoid making any unnecessary lines. Detail things in, on, around, and sticking out from under snow areas, rather than the snow itself. Let your white paper work for you.

Because of limited hours of light in winter, some scenes cannot be finished in one day's sitting. This panorama was sketched in two parts: first the right side, then the left, on two consecutive days.

In this woods the snow was waist deep. My snowshoes made a nice platform upon which I perched to work.

Stains and marks on tree bark can be suggested by pressing your kneadable eraser here and there on the already shaded areas of trees. Each pressing will lift off an irregularly shaped light spot.

Track of White-footed Mouse
in deep snow
Jim Arnosky
Jan. 28 '87

26

The course of shadows on the snow indicates the shape of the land under the snow. Some shadows are sharp-edged silhouettes. Others are more diffused. Show this difference in your sketches.

By midwinter the snow in the woods was over three feet deep. The going there was rough. Tracks of large animals, such as deer and coyotes, became scarce. Only the smaller animals, those light enough to travel over the snow without sinking all the way down, were out and about.

This track of a white-footed mouse shows the little creature's entire body shape, including its tail. Imagine the effort it takes to hop when each and every landing sinks you up to your nose in snow!

After two nights of twenty-eight degrees below zero Fahrenheit, and another of minus sixteen, I made a visit to a favorite local spring. The look and sound of its running water assured me that, no matter how awful the cold was outdoors, the earth beneath the snow had not frozen solid.

This site is high on a hillside. Softwoods stand all around. The spring has been piped downhill and pours into a wide wooden barrel. The barrel is half buried in snow and locked in its place by overflowing water, which has formed into ice all around the barrel's girth. It is a watering spot for man and beast. Thirsty pilgrims have kept a path to it tramped down in the snow.

Woodland Spring
JEO Jan 30/87

29

*The charm or power of a sketch made quickly lies in its
hurried look and the boldness of its line strokes.*

It was the last half hour of daylight. Deanna had the table set.
I decided to go out on my snowshoes to see what kind of sketch
I could do in the fifteen minutes or so before supper would be
ready. This view of Ramtails, as seen from the brushy border of
our brook, is what I came back with.

Quick sketch before supper —
The farm as seen from the brook
along the stream — J.W.
Feb 2, 187

31

I sketched this snowy owl as I saw it magnified twenty times through my spotting scope. The owl was perched high on the snow-covered rooftop of an industrial building in Barre, Vermont. It is good fortune to have such a creature wintering here. Snowy owls usually do not travel so far south from their arctic range.

Most of the time I was sketching, the owl was facing away from me. Whenever it did swivel its head and stare downward in my direction, its cool yellow eyes—eyes that can spot and sharply define a mouse a hundred yards distant—scrutinized me and my every movement.

When you are sketching a living bird, work fast. Your subject may fly away at any moment. Concentrate on the bird's overall form rather than its anatomical structure. Try to capture its pose.

After you have sketched the bird's full figure, you can begin looking and drawing in more detail.

Do not bother looking for and drawing individual feathers. Instead, suggest feathered areas—the head, breast, flanks, back, wings, and tail.

Add any stripes, spots, light-colored patches, broad dark areas, and other field markings that you see.

Snowy Owl - Barre VT.
Jim Arnosky
Feb '77
(wind blowing up feathers on breast)

33

A living bird is almost always a quick study. Every once in a while you will find outdoors a killed animal that can be examined up close for as long as you wish. Bird artists have long benefited from the misfortunes of their subjects.

This ruffed grouse had been struck down in flight by an automobile. Many of its rump feathers were knocked off by the blow. Its tail feathers, though, were intact and revealed the interrupted black bar that identifies the female of this species. (In the male ruffed grouse the black bar is solid all across the tail.)

During a bout with flu I spent most of my time indoors studying and drawing this bird, feather by feather.

Now is the time to look at and carefully draw every feather in its proper place.

The more you learn about feathers—their various shapes, textures, and how they lie to cover and protect a bird's body—the easier it becomes to draw birds.

To make feathers look wafer thin, keep your pencil point sharp and make all outlines very light.

Each individual feather's pattern plays some part in a bird's overall markings. For example, what you see in the field as a long white stripe along a bird's side is actually many feathers, each with a small streak of white, aligned in a way that creates a long white stripe.

For making light mottling on dark feather areas, use a kneadable eraser to lift off blotches of graphite.

NOTE: **Do not handle dead animals more than necessary. Wash your hands after each sketching session. Store the model securely wrapped in a freezer.**

Underwing
(No markings all ditc)

Details of Ruffed Grouse ♀
— drawn from road killed bird —
Jim Arnosky
Feb 9, 1987

Cornstalks sticking
up out of 3' of snowcover
Ryegate Corner, VT.
very cold 10° / 20 MPH wind
wind chill – 24°
                    JE
                    Feb. 10, 1987
too cold to sketch!
– a droplet of my condensed breath
froze as soon as it hit the paper –

frozen
drops
of
my breath

36

As soon as I was well, I headed outdoors to sketch again in the open air. I went to a high and windy place called Ryegate Corner. There, blowing snow is heaped into deep drifts across rolling farmland. In one snow-whitened field I noticed a few cornstalks missed in the autumn harvest. At the top of one stalk a long, dry corn leaf hung flapping in the wind. I made my way through the deep snow to that cornstalk flag, squatted down in a drift, and began to sketch.

But it was simply too cold to be outdoors sketching. Wind was whipping over the field at twenty miles per hour, blasting me head-on. Combined with the already bitter cold air temperature (ten degrees), that wind created a chill factor of minus twenty-four degrees. Unbearable. I quickly gave in and left the scene. On windy days I now consider the wind-chill factor before going outdoors to sketch. (A wind-chill chart is provided on page 48.)

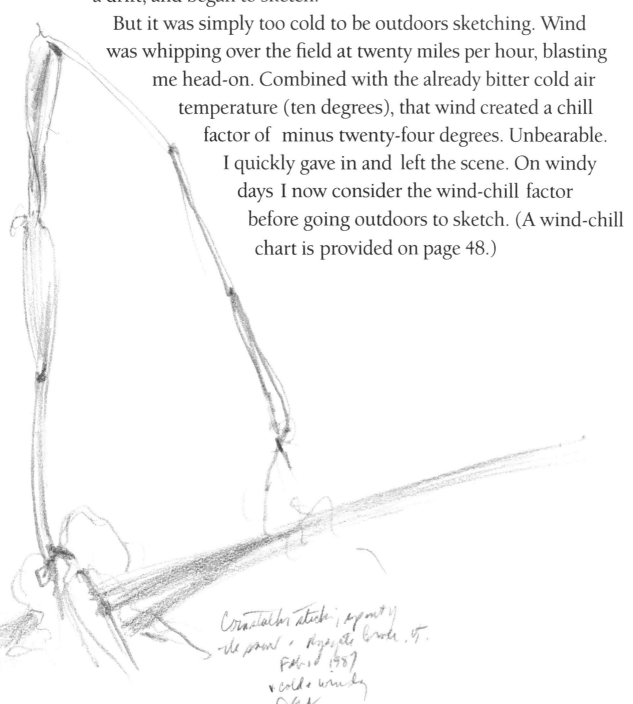

Cornstalks sticking up out of the snow · Ryegate Corner, Vt. Feb. 1987 · cold & windy

Mt. Vista and Snow Fields
Bible Hill Road
John Arno...
Feb 87

While driving back home after attempting to sketch the corn-stalks, I stopped to enjoy (from inside my warm vehicle) this mountain vista. The mountains, which are in nearby New Hampshire, loom up over a snow-covered Vermont hill.

A few weeks later, on a considerably warmer afternoon, I returned to the spot and set up my easel on the roadside. As I sketched, three crows calling loudly to one another winged through the scene. They too seemed to be enjoying the milder weather.

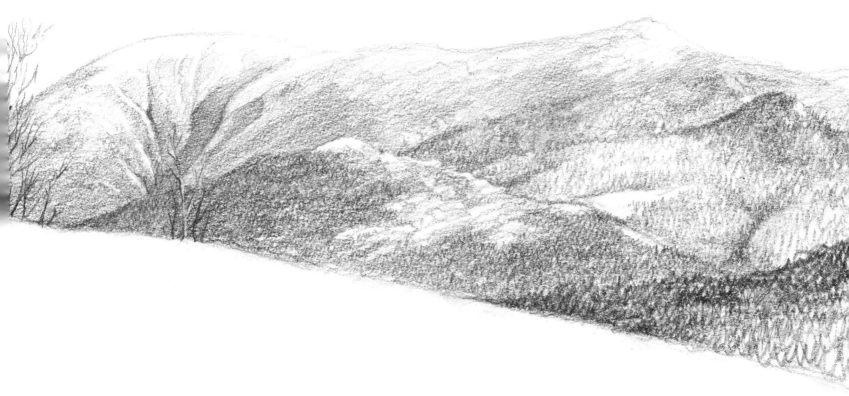

Notice which trees have rounded or oval crowns and which trees terminate in less organized designs.

After you have sketched in the trunk and crown shape of a tree, add the lines for the limbs, each emanating from the tree's trunk. Then resharpen your pencil point and add the smaller branches that emanate from the limbs.

When sketching distant mountains, keep your shading lines light. Shading too dark will bring the mountains forward and spoil the feeling of depth and distance in the picture.

As you draw, keep in mind that each wrinkle you see in a mountain's surface is a hollow of land. Every white patch on its slopes or summit is a field of snow. Dark tree areas are evergreen forests. Lighter tree areas are stands of hardwoods.

This drawing was made during another of our really cold spells—subzero at night and temperatures barely climbing to the teens during the day. In the protection of the woods through which this trout stream flows, there was no wind and consequently no chill factor to compound the cold.

Most of the brook's surface was encased in ice and buried under deep snow. In places where the water ran out in the open, the surrounding snow cover hung over the stream bank like thick white icing on the edge of a cake.

In deeply cold weather I sketch using a very soft lead (a 6B pencil). I have found that very soft lead enables me to draw smoothly, even during those bone-chilling moments when my hand shivers a bit.

Each stratum in the snowbank represents one compressed layer of crystals accumulated from one storm. Count the layers in this snowbank and you will know approximately the number of snowfalls we have had so far this winter.

Water in snowy country often looks black. White snow reflects so much light, it prevents light from penetrating the water's surface. This stream in snowless times is brightly illuminated.

Despite how black the water looked, I could still see some boulders in the stream bed. A few touches of my eraser were all that was needed to suggest them in my drawing.

Trout brook in Winter
Jim Arnosky
Feb 12, 1987

41

Yoko is our Alaskan husky. She lives outdoors all winter long, preferring the cold porch to our warm kitchen. That's the wolf in her. Yoko sleeps curled up, nose to tail, in a misshapen old wicker chair. When it storms, snow blows in and covers her in whiteness. On clear cold mornings frost forms on her coat.

This afternoon I caught Yoko napping and scribbled her portrait before she woke up and ran over to greet me.

Yoko asleep on porch chair
-4° Feb 15, 1987

This dog sleeps this way in all
temperatures ... last night at
30 below I peeked out and saw
her sleeping calmly ... not a shiver!

43

In late winter we visit the barn often. It is the time of the year when our sheep's lambs are due. This winter, Blueberry, one of our dark brown ewes, was the first to lamb. She gave birth to twins. Both were creamy white in color. It was a very cold morning on which to be born. I made this sketch only minutes after the second lamb emerged. The newborns were still wet from birth. Their little warm bodies steamed in the frigid air.

Blueberry's Twins - just born
9 am sunny morning (-10°) colder in Barn
JBL Feb 16 1991

4½ hrs. old
and resting

this 3½ hrs. old
is still groggy.

*When you sketch very young animals, try to capture the fresh
outlook in their eyes.*

8 hrs old
Both lambs alert

John Christmas
Feb 16 1987

45

Never stare directly at the sun, not even during sunset when its light appears less intense.

To sketch a sunset, arrive at your scene an hour or so before the sun is to go down. This will give you time to block in the landscape. Then, as the sun dips nearer to the horizon, begin your shading and work until dark settles in.

Here, the town plow has hurled chunks of snow onto an already high bank as it cleared off the shoulders of our road. Another day is ending. The sun is going down, leaving us again in deepening cold. Tonight, as on so many previous nights, the temperature will drop well below zero.

But the cold cannot last much longer. Tomorrow the sun will rise a little earlier and set a little later. Each new day's few additional minutes of warm sunlight will help pry loose winter's grip. Someday soon it will be spring.

47

WIND-CHILL CHART

On days when it is windy and cold, consult this chart. It will help you determine whether or not it is prudent to go sketching outdoors.

Wind Speed (mph)	*Actual Air Temperature (Degrees Fahrenheit)*									
calm	35°	30°	25°	20°	15°	10°	5°	0°	−5°	−10°
5	33	27	21	19	12	7	0	−5	−10	−15
10	22	16	10	3	−3	−9	−15	−22	−27	−34
15	16	9	2	−5	−11	−18	−25	−31	−38	−45
20	12	4	−3	−10	−17	−24	−31	−39	−46	−53
25	8	1	−7	−15	−22	−29	−36	−44	−51	−58
30	6	−2	−10	−18	−25	−33	−41	−49	−56	−64
35	4	−4	−12	−20	−27	−35	−43	−52	−58	−67
40	3	−5	−13	−21	−29	−37	−45	−53	−60	−69
45	2	−6	−14	−22	−30	−38	−46	−54	−62	−70

Equivalent temperature produced by wind chill